You've developed a
top-notch business plan.

Now what?

It's time to execute.

THE TRIANGLE STRATEGY

How to Create a Culture
of Engagement and Execution

Michael R. Tull

The Triangle Strategy™ is a service mark of Michael Tull for consulting services in the field of performance management.

ISBN-10: 1477562834
ISBN-13: 978-1477562833

Book design by Dan Selzer at Sheffield Product, Queens, NY

Dedicated to Selma and Nathan Tull

TABLE OF CONTENTS

APPENDIX

WHY THIS BOOK?

If you watched the 2012 London Olympics, you saw the Jamaican sprinter, Usain Bolt, continue to dominate the 100- and 200-meter events as he did in 2008. You also saw Michael Phelps maintain his gold-medal position after winning eight gold medals in Beijing. Watching these two men perform to the highest levels, you witnessed the culmination of years of training and discipline that had honed their physical and mental abilities, allowing each to excel at his sport.

One objective of *The Triangle Strategy* is to show that, as on the playing field, discipline is required by everyone in the workplace if we expect to build organizations that excel. It will delve into the fundamental actions that must be honed in order to successfully compete in the marketplace.

Over the last number of years, books, articles, and research organizations have brought attention to the concept of *employee engagement* as a critical element for creating a successful business. In 2006, The Conference Board, a global business research organization, conducted a review of the literature and major research studies in the field. In seven studies on overall engagement levels, they found that only 21–52 percent of employees were engaged.[1]

Although The Conference Board states that it is complicated to compare the studies because they include a wide array of engagement definitions and research methods, some patterns did emerge. If its findings are compared with widely accepted insights of those who study high performance in organizations, a clear path for developing an effective workplace appears. The research and literature suggest that employees become engaged and perform better when they:

▲ Have *open, trusting relationships* with their managers

▲ Are *appropriately challenged* by day-to-day work and are *given opportunities for growth*

▲ Have *clear targets* that are *valued as contributing* toward achieving business goals

▲ Feel that their *opinions count* and are *taken into consideration* in decision making

▲ Receive *regular feedback* on their performance and are *recognized for successes*

This list is not new to anyone who reads leadership and management literature. These characteristics are regularly identified as being fundamental to engaged, high-performing organizations. It seems, however, that managers do not have a clear understanding of how to create this kind of workplace.

---

1. Conference Board Report, *Employee Engagement, A Review of Current Research and Its Implications,* Research Report E-0010-06-RR, 2006.

In March 2010, members of the Harvard Business Review Advisory Council surveyed a representative group of 1,075 *Review* readers for their insights about strategy and execution in their organizations. One significant finding was that making strategy meaningful to frontline workers was thought to be the greatest execution challenge. This concern broadens the discussion from employee engagement and the relatively soft topics of employee retention, motivation, and satisfaction to include business execution and operational excellence.

The purpose of *The Triangle Strategy* is to provide managers and the people who work for them with a clear understanding of what is required to create a high-performing workplace. Its focus is on engagement as well as execution. It picks up where strategy development leaves off: the point at which the organization relies on the effectiveness of individuals and groups to implement its plans. Though many companies develop smart, strategic plans, many do not pay equal attention to the discipline and focus required for day-to-day execution.

I set out to write a practical guide for managers. However, since success relies on the relationship and cooperation that exists between leaders and their teams, I realized that this book works as an operational guide for both groups. *The Triangle Strategy* will provide new and experienced managers with a framework for assessing and improving their management practices, while also providing those who report to them guidelines to be effective in their role.

THE TRIANGLE STRATEGY

As organizations respond to changes in economic and competitive conditions, it's more important than ever to understand the fundamentals required to create and maintain an engaged, execution-focused workforce. The aim of the Triangle Strategy is to unravel the complexities of the performance process. It takes well-known best practices for managing and leading and organizes them into a model that is both practical and useful.

The idea for this book was planted a few years ago when I coached George, an information technology expert for an international bank who had recently been promoted into a team leader role. In our first session, George mentioned that he wasn't sure he wanted to take on the supervisory position. *"I understand systems,"* he said, *"but I don't understand people. Can you give me a system for managing people?"*

Good question. I had been in the management development field for over twenty-five years as a manager, consultant, trainer, and coach, but the performance models I knew seemed too complex. George needed a simple framework that could be applied easily. I said I'd give it some more thought.

At subsequent meetings, I introduced George to a systematic approach for leading his group. It was a three-phase process that combined accepted leadership and management practices. I suggested that he start by setting expectations, then provide support while allowing people space to do their work, and finally, give feedback about their performance. This process made sense to him and, during our work together, he became comfortable with this sequenced approach. George decided to accept the job, and I learned from his manager that he was doing very well.

The set of management practices that I had introduced to George was sufficient to get him started in his new role. However, I recognized that this was only the first piece of the puzzle, and that a more comprehensive strategy was required for him to become truly effective.

THE TRIANGLE

My discussion with George started me on a path to identify the critical elements that impact day-to-day operational performance. Gradually, by reviewing the literature and discussing performance issues with clients and colleagues, the Triangle Strategy—a high-performance model for managing—began taking shape.

It soon became clear that all work in organizations includes four key elements: 1) *Leaders* who set direction, 2) *Performers* who execute the work of the organization, 3) *Tasks* that need to be done, and 4) *Goals* toward which all work activity is focused. The Triangle below illustrates the relationship between the four elements.

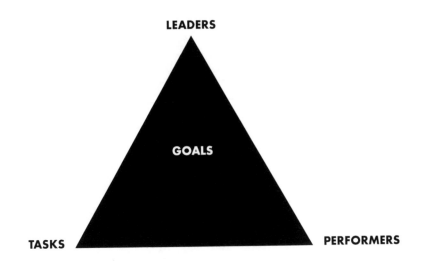

Next I asked myself: *When an organization is functioning at a high level, how would each of these elements be characterized?* An examination of leadership and management best practices suggested additions to the Triangle as follows.

Goals

Well-defined goals include three components: a purpose, a target, and balance. *Purpose* identifies the business reason for the goal—why it's a worthwhile challenge. *Target* defines what needs to be accomplished and the time frame in which to do it. *Balance* suggests that consideration be given to the full spectrum of outcome measures to avoid unintended results.

Leaders

The practices of setting expectations, providing support, and giving feedback are required skills for anyone taking on a leadership role. *Setting expectations* is the first step in establishing who is responsible for achieving a goal. It sets up the rules of play: what people can expect from each other. As the work progresses, leaders switch to *providing support*—being available for assistance and encouragement and to recognize progress. Finally, through *giving feedback*, leaders let people know how their performance is being perceived.

Performers

Performers are defined by a set of characteristics: fit, interest, and ability to self-manage. They should be the right *fit* for a position, having, or being able to obtain, the skills, knowledge, and experience to do the work while also possessing the intellectual, psychological, and physical abilities to fill the role. A leading indicator of a performer's effectiveness is the *interest* they have in their work—whether they can see value in what they're being asked to accomplish. Finally, they need a talent for *self-management*, which is the ability to manage time, tasks and priorities.

Tasks

Tasks are further defined by three elements that impact the performance process: workflow, obstacles, and consequences. *Workflow* represents how tasks are done—the steps and actions required to do the work or complete an assignment. *Obstacles* represent the barriers that could impede work. *Consequences* refer to the potential positive or negative effects that performers experience from doing their work.

Although more complete as it now stands, the Triangle represents a static view of the workplace, when in fact it's a dynamic environment in which there is constant learning and adaptation. In order to represent this learning process, three arrows have been added that suggest leaders and performers need to continually be asking the question *"How can we do things better?"*

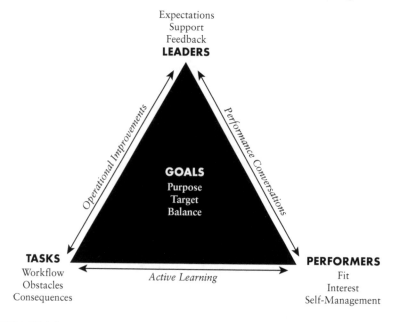

The arrow between *Leaders* and *Performers* represents the core *performance conversations* that need to take place: setting expectations, providing support, and giving feedback. The arrow suggests that these are two-way conversations, the aim being to stimulate discussions in which thoughts and ideas are shared openly.

The arrow between *Performers* and *Tasks* represents an *active learning* mindset, a process of discovery that encourages performers to reflect on their actions and results, and use insights to improve their effectiveness.

The arrow between *Leaders* and *Tasks* represents management's continued attention to making *operational improvements*. Leaders assess operational results on a regular basis and remain vigilant for opportunities to fine-tune how the organization functions.

The difference between active learning and operational improvements is that active learning, for the most part, aims at short-term adjustments and immediate impact. Conversely, operational improvements may address more complex issues—such as policies and procedures, organizational structure, and workplace culture—that can have long-term consequences on a broad spectrum of work activities.

The Triangle represents a universal performance strategy. Regardless of whether the organization is an outdoor greenmarket, a local restaurant, or a corporate headquarters, it will have these features. Despite the different façades, you will observe people functioning in *leader* and *performer* roles, working on a series of *tasks* directed toward achieving specific *goals*. If you are striving for a high-performing operational culture, all of the Triangle elements need to be in place. Every degree you are removed from the optimum reduces the competitiveness of your organization.

APPLICATION

The power of the Triangle lies in its application. This book presents the Triangle as a theoretical construct, but its benefits can only be truly recognized through its use. Below are two methods for applying the Triangle: as a guide to inform management actions, and as an analytical tool to assist in the planning process.

A Guide for Actions

The Triangle framework provides a structure for implementing new initiatives. Whether leading a change effort or delegating an assignment, the Triangle suggests using the following as a guide:

Goals	Define the purpose of the initiative and its value to the organization. Ensure the target and time frames are clear, and measures for success are balanced.
Leaders	Manage the initiative through performance conversations. Talk about the purpose of the goals and their benefits to the organization. Collaborate in developing a set of cohesive action plans. Schedule follow-up meetings to monitor and celebrate progress. Give meaningful feedback.
Performers	Make sure performers are prepared to carry out the initiative. Provide support and development opportunities if needed. Discuss how to include new assignments into their present workload.
Tasks	Assess the complexity of the tasks. Make every effort to streamline the work process and reduce or remove barriers. Discuss potential positive and/or negative consequences.
Active Learning	Emphasize the need for people to identify ways to become more efficient and effective.
Operational Improvements	Consider the organization's existing policies, procedures, structure, and culture. Take actions to improve the likelihood of success.

Essentially, you can use the above as an execution checklist. These actions may seem to be common sense. Unfortunately, they are not common practice. In order to create a highly effective workplace, everyone in the organization needs to make these practices a routine and normal part of the organization's operational fabric.

An Analytical & Planning Tool

There is a better chance of accomplishing your goals if the work to be done is considered through the lens of the Triangle. When I've shown colleagues and managers the Triangle, they have found that it provides a quick way to frame and discuss performance issues. Focusing on the Triangle elements helps you hone in on the variables—both positive and negative—that will have the most significant impact on results.

The Triangle does not provide answers but directs you toward the right questions. For instance, the following questions highlight issues to consider when planning a change process.

Goals	*What goals do we want to achieve?*
	Does everyone have a clear understanding of our target and time frame?
	Are our measures of success balanced to avoid unintentional results?
Leaders	*Have our expectations been made clear?*
	Do we know what people are expecting of us in leading this initiative?
	Have we scheduled regular meetings to monitor progress, provide feedback, and make adjustments to plans if necessary?

Performers	*Are staff members prepared to make the needed changes?*
	What is their interest level in achieving the goals?
	Have we been able to shift priorities to balance the new workload? Are there any distractions?
Tasks	*Are we clear about the tasks involved? Can they be organized more effectively?*
	Have we eliminated or reduced any obstacles that could interfere with success?
	Will staff members experience positive or negative consequences from performing in the new way?
Operational Improvements	*Do we need to adjust policies, procedures, or our organizational structure in order to execute the change effectively?*

Use these questions to prepare to introduce and manage the change process. Their use with project teams or groups of direct reports can help to create a common understanding of the implementation challenges.

The best way to understand how the Triangle works is to try it out. It is through the process of working with the Triangle that it will become meaningful and valuable. Examples of its application are provided in the Appendix.

PULLING IT ALL TOGETHER

The Triangle embodies a comprehensive framework for creating a workplace culture in which everyone is engaged and focused on implementing operational plans. The reality, in most organizations, is that not all the Triangle elements are in place. Goals are not always clear; leaders don't always provide necessary feedback; performers are not always the right fit for their positions. Leaders and performers often need development and nurturing. The Triangle points to where attention is needed.

Learning to use the Triangle helps clarify the performance process so you are better able to focus your actions and schedule your time. Although these concepts may not be new to experienced managers, the Triangle provides a framework that will keep them at the forefront of our minds.

The real benefits come from applying the Triangle. As you continue reading, you may find certain sections more meaningful than others, based on your role in the organization. Whether you're delegating an assignment, initiating a change, or starting a new team, the Triangle helps focus on the actions that will achieve the most effective results.

PERFORMANCE GOALS

Organizations are formed for reasons that may be as diverse as creating the next hot app for smartphones, franchising a chain of restaurants, or reducing world hunger. What organizations have in common is that in order to succeed, they need a distinct set of goals— a clear view of what needs to be achieved.

Goals provide the stake in the ground. Whether it's a straightforward goal like creating a monthly update report, or one that is broad and complex, such as implementing a new technology system, goals focus attention on what's important and provide direction for taking action.

GOAL STATEMENT CRITERIA

The performance process starts with deciding what you want to achieve and writing it as a performance goal that will spur action. Well-defined goal statements are written to include three elements: 1) purpose, 2) target, and 3) balance.

Purpose

In order to get support for a goal, you need to communicate why it's imperative to spend the time and effort to achieve it. As President Barack Obama said in his jobs speech to the nation on September 8, 2011:

Tonight we meet at an urgent time for our country. We continue to face an economic crisis that has left millions of our neighbors jobless, and a political crisis that has made things worse . . . The purpose of the American Jobs Act is simple: to put more people back to work and more money in the pockets of those who are working.

"Pass this bill," he urged. Whether or not you agreed with Obama's solution, his purpose for passing the bill was well defined: to create jobs.

The exhortation to act is a common refrain in daily operations of any competitive organization. Whether asking people to work longer hours or adapt to more complex technology, it's important that the purpose behind these requests is both compelling and clear.

Target

Goals are effectively written when everyone has the same understanding of what they mean. To this end, each goal will have a clear target—a vision of the result and a time component. The vision defines what you want to achieve; the time frame provides milestones and end points. For instance, in a speech before congress in 1961, John F. Kennedy famously challenged the nation with a goal of putting a man on the moon by the end of the decade. Both his vision and time frame were clear.

Ideally, you want a challenge to involve the right amount of tension, with time parameters that don't cause unnecessary stress or careless work, but still provide a sense of urgency.

Balance

The notion of balance permeates our lives. We are encouraged to eat healthy food, but not in excess. Exercise, but don't overdo it. Protect our children, but prepare them to become independent. The objective is to guard against unintended consequences. The part of the Kennedy quote that is often left out is *". . . and returning him safely to earth."*

The critical element in creating balanced goals is to identify a set of measures that can guard against lopsided results. For instance, if your goal is to have an assignment completed by the end of the week—a rushed project because of a client's time constraints—you also want to emphasize the desire for error-free results.

For example, on February 24, 2010, Toyota executives were called before a congressional committee that was investigating reasons for excessive recall of some Toyota models. According to *Bloomsberg Businessweek*, they had gotten ". . . carried away chasing high-speed growth, market share, and productivity gains."[2] This suggests that they had lost sight of the commitment to quality embedded in Toyota's corporate culture and inadvertently sacrificed it in their quest to succeed.

This case shows how well-balanced goals require a clear understanding of the organization as a system—how pushing one lever may have an impact on other areas of the business.

Following is a detailed goal that was used for starting up a new department in a consumer research organization. It required the efforts of a high-level cross-functional team.

---

2. Alan Ohnsman, Jeff Green, and Kae Inoue, "The Humbling of Toyota," *Bloomberg BusinessWeek*, March 22 & 29, 2010: 33–36.

Purpose: Streamline operational functions to maximize efficiencies of distributing research content to multiple digital channels.

Target: Centralize numerous operational functions, tasks, and processes into a newly created Content Operations Department that will be operational by the end of the second quarter.

Balance: Our initial success will be measured by our ability to:

▲ Increase productivity by developing tools to automate the production and delivery of content

▲ Promote accountability by clearly defining roles and responsibilities for specific tasks

▲ Eliminate manual processes that impact productivity and result in errors

▲ Implement high levels of quality control.

Notice that the focus of this goal statement is solely on results. It does not include any action steps. The specific plans to achieve the goal were discussed and worked out in a number of subsequent conversations.

PULLING IT ALL TOGETHER

The best goals challenge us and focus attention on adding value to the organization. By taking the time to think through goals in terms of purpose, target, and balance, managers will have a broad understanding of what needs to be discussed with those designated to carry out the work. Goals open and close the performance cycle. They provide the impetus for work and a reason to celebrate when successfully achieved. Well-communicated and well-monitored goals provide the guiding force that galvanizes day-to-day operations.

PERFORMANCE CONVERSATIONS

The three performance conversations—setting expectations, providing support, and giving feedback—represent the most impactful element in the Triangle. Providing the foundation for all performance-based discussions between leaders and performers, they take place over the course of the performance process and are inextricably linked. Each discussion has a specific purpose, and the quality of these conversations has much to do with how engaged and productive people are in the workplace.

This chapter introduces these conversations, providing guidelines for conducting them effectively. Following chapters offer a more in-depth perspective from the leader and performer points of view.

THE CONVERSATIONS

Setting Expectations

Setting expectations is the initial conversation in the performance process. It's a leader's opportunity to ignite performer interest in the work. How well these conversations are conducted can determine the level of performance that people achieve. The aim is for leaders and performers to come to an agreement about goals, and collaborate on figuring out how tasks will be accomplished.

Whether delegating a routine assignment or initiating a change, the objective of these conversations is the same: to establish clear action steps and operating parameters, ownership of an assignment, and a schedule for monitoring and providing support. The following is a framework for conducting these conversations. Although this is not a script, it's recommended that these topics flow as outlined.

Goals	Clarify goals to ensure that everyone involved understands the purpose and aims of the assignment.
Benefits	Highlight the value of achieving the goal—what it will mean to the performers, their teams, and/or the organization.
Actions	Create a set of action plans that performers can own. Include task assignments, due dates, and a schedule for progress review meetings.
Obstacles	Identify potential barriers that might impede the implementation. Discuss how to eliminate the obstructions or reduce their impact. Adjust plans if necessary.

The purpose of setting expectations is to stimulate interest in achieving a goal and start assignments off on the right track. In doing so, these discussions provide the foundation for future support and feedback conversations.

Providing Support

Although performers are responsible for an assignment when they take it on, support conversations are meant to help them along. When *providing support*, the objective is to offer assistance and encouragement as well as recognize progress—to discuss how things are going and prevent surprises as deadlines approach. These may be informal, stop-by-your-desk conversations or scheduled meetings.

Although informal conversations can be appropriate when experienced people are doing routine tasks, scheduled meetings are built into implementation plans when performers require close attention or when lengthy assignments need to be monitored over a period of time. The following framework can help guide either type of conversation.

Review	Check progress against plans; compare to expectations and deliverables.
Assess	Acknowledge what has been done well; call attention to areas needing improvement.
Learn	Discuss ideas for working more effectively.
Adjust	If needed, change the implementation plans.

This structure can help you address a number of important performance issues in a short amount of time. The objective is to resolve problems, bolster performer confidence, and maintain forward momentum.

Giving Feedback

Setting expectations starts the performance process, *support conversations* keep the system humming, and *giving feedback* keeps people on the right track. The most effective feedback loops back to and strengthens the original expectations. In general, it has the most impact when given soon after the behavior has been observed.

People spend a lot of time at their jobs, and they work hard. They deserve to know how their work is being perceived. In that respect, all feedback, both *positive* and *corrective*, is constructive.

Positive feedback reinforces good performance; it tells people to keep doing what they've been doing. It recognizes a person's ability and contributions to the organization, provides encouragement, and demonstrates that efforts are appreciated.

Corrective feedback guides those who need to adjust behavior; it steers them back onto the right path. Without corrective feedback, people may be doing tasks incorrectly, inadvertently wasting time and energy. Corrective feedback has two phases:

Phase I is normal feedback that brings attention to actions that need to change. In most instances, this will be sufficient.

Phase II is called for if improvements are not made after multiple feedback meetings. During these corrective conversations, you are essentially putting performers on warning.

Some managers are uncomfortable conducting these conversations. That's understandable; feedback meetings can be emotional. Whether giving positive or corrective feedback, the following framework will provide a structure for these discussions.

Observations	Share what you have noticed about a person's performance and its impact on the assignment or other team members. Use data or facts to reinforce your feedback.
Reactions	Before you move forward, allow time to discuss the performer's point of view.
Exploration	In the case of corrective feedback, collaborate in figuring out how to get back on track.
Solutions	Agree on a plan of corrective action.

For organizations to be truly successful, it is important that feedback becomes a routine part of the operating culture and, as such, provides a critical mechanism for achieving goals.

Although each performance conversation has a distinct purpose, they often work in tandem. For instance, support conversations provide opportunities to give positive feedback. Similarly, feedback conversations become vehicles for reviewing and possibly resetting expectations.

Performance conversations represent the core set of practices that managers must develop if they want to build teams that excel in operational execution. When conducted effectively, these meetings become a mechanism for fostering open, trusting work relationships.

GUIDING PRINCIPLES

Performance conversations provide the foundation for creating effective leader-performer partnerships. Years of experience, reinforced by the prevailing business literature, suggest that there are three guiding principles that can help make these meetings productive.

Aim for Two-Way Conversations

In two-way conversations, each party is open to hearing the other's point of view. Such conversations provide opportunities to get a better understanding of what others know and how they think. These are collaborative discussions that encourage people to express opinions and ask questions. The objective is to engage all parties in order to bring out the best ideas and develop ownership for decisions. It is widely accepted that when people are engaged in discussions about work and feel that their ideas are being considered, personal responsibility begins to flourish.

Consider Individual and Organizational Needs

It is not uncommon that organizational goals become the focus at the expense of individual needs. In order to build an engaged, productive workforce, you need to create a balance. Performers who give their best effort will continue working at that level if they feel the organization is also helping them reach their personal goals. Keeping this in mind increases the likelihood of satisfying the needs of both the organization and the performer.

Remain Goal-Focused

Performance conversations often do not follow a direct line from start to finish. They can be complex and emotional, possibly causing a conversation to veer off on tangents and lose focus. In order to use time effectively, leaders and performers need to concentrate on the purpose for the meeting. A clear goal provides the hook for reining in wandering discussions and keeping conversations on topic.

These guiding principles provide the foundational set of values for conducting effective performance conversations. They bring attention to both the human and business sides of the organization by encouraging engagement while keeping the focus on execution.

THREE-PHASE MEETING STRUCTURE

Performance conversations are often complicated and include details that may send you off course. This three-phase structure—setup, discussion, and summary—is a useful framework for maintaining focus on what you want to accomplish in these meetings.

Setup	Begin by stating the purpose, agenda, and time frame for the meeting. The objective is to let participants know why the meeting has been organized and what they can expect. It prepares everyone for the coming discussion.
Discussion	In the second phase, participants hash out problems, develop solutions, and make decisions.
Summary	The final phase is used to ensure that participants agree to action plans and are prepared to move forward. Establish a time to meet again to review progress.

Each phase in this structure has an objective. The setup frames the conversation. The discussion is where the work of the meeting is done. The summary brings it all together. And although meetings are organized around specific goals, they are also opportunities to boost performer confidence.

PULLING IT ALL TOGETHER

Many of our organizations today are high-pressure, do-more-with-less workplaces. Everyone is being asked to stretch. Having open discussions about goals and how to achieve them has always been important, but now it is critical. A disciplined approach to these conversations highlights vital issues and inevitably adds to the organization's ability to succeed.

This chapter introduced a systematic framework for conducting performance conversations. *Setting expectations* clarifies goals and action plans; *providing support* guides the work along; and *giving feedback* keeps performers on the right path. Once you decide which conversation to have, consider the guiding principles that are important to include in the meeting. The three-phase meeting structure helps you organize your thoughts.

Experienced managers will recognize these conversations. They include a set of management practices that have been assessed, refined, and written about numerous times over the last fifty-plus years. Although most managers are familiar with these practices, the research on employee engagement suggests that they are not being used effectively. The topics covered in this chapter should help you control and focus these discussions.

THE LEADER'S ROLE

The word "leader" is not used on organizational charts, but it is a role that falls to many within the organization. As defined by the Triangle, a leader can be anyone who delegates work to others. Executives and managers fall into this category through the requirements of their position. Performers on the frontline also take on the leader role when asked to head up a project team.

The Triangle suggests that whether the leader is a manager or a frontline employee acting in a leadership capacity, certain behaviors are required to be effective. These behaviors include: 1) conducting effective performance conversations, and 2) continually seeking ways to make operational improvements.

PERFORMANCE CONVERSATIONS: THE LEADER'S PERSPECTIVE

The three performance conversations discussed earlier—setting expectations, providing support, and giving feedback—provide leaders with opportunities to engage performers in discussions about an assignment, reduce any anxieties about doing the work, and instill a sense of ownership for the outcome. Just as importantly, they are the vehicles for creating effective leader-performer relationships that are built on a framework of mutual respect, openness, and trust.

The Expectations Conversation

The aim of setting expectations is to gain agreement about goals and implementation plans. The conversation may cover immediate tasks that need to be done or take a broader view to establish how teams or department groups will conduct themselves.

An example of the latter involved Aiden, a senior-level middle manager in a global financial institution stationed in New York. He was passed over for a promotion, and a manager from the London office was assigned as his boss. Aiden understood why he hadn't gotten the position, but was unsure about what his new boss expected from him. In coaching sessions, we discussed his concerns. He decided to ask his new boss for a meeting to discuss their expectations of each other.

The new manager's response was telling. He told Aiden that he was not interested in discussing expectations because it was "Management 101 stuff." In other words, it was something he'd been taught and had used at the beginning of his career, but no longer felt was important. It was a missed opportunity for these two experienced managers to discuss their goals and interests and find common ground. I saw Aiden a few months later, and things were still unsettled in the department.

Whether meeting with someone who is starting a new job or delegating an assignment, establishing expectations is a critical discussion. It helps people to get grounded quickly and focuses attention on the work that needs to be done. It's the first step in building an effective working relationship.

The Support Conversation

Support conversations are opportunities to discuss any issues that may be inhibiting staff performance. They provide a forum for reviewing incremental results, responding to performer concerns, and ensuring projects remain on track. Your aim is for performers to leave these meetings feeling energized and focused in the right direction.

A major aspect of the leader role is to provide support when needed. It's crucial that people feel comfortable coming to you when they're unsure about doing tasks correctly or how to proceed. Timely conversations when performers have these kinds of questions can significantly reduce anxiety levels and prevent wasted effort.

The Feedback Conversation

Feedback conversations focus on reinforcing expectations that were established in the initial performance discussions. To be effective, they should become a routine part of your working relationships, rather than being reserved for semiannual or annual performance reviews.

A major oversight that managers often admit to is not giving positive feedback when it's deserved. Good employees are often taken for granted. An example is Jennifer, a cook at a popular Chicago restaurant. She gets up early to work twelve-hour days for a low hourly wage. She enjoys and is motivated by the work, the camaraderie that can exist in a kitchen, and hearing that people enjoy her food. Whether you're a chef or office manager, you can't buy that kind of motivation. If you want to keep performers like Jennifer, it's important to recognize their effort and acknowledge a job well done.

Giving feedback, especially corrective feedback, can be an intimidating activity for many people. This was the case for a participant in one of my training programs who was a fairly new manager to his current team. Although his team was comprised of highly experienced and skilled technicians, and their work was continually thorough and correct, they routinely missed deadlines.

This manager was younger than his team, with less time in the organization. Through discussions in my class, he recognized that as a result of his timidity, he had avoided giving the team feedback that their lateness had become a problem, so it was thought to be acceptable. When he raised the issue with them and reset the deadline expectations, the team quickly resolved the problem.

Research conducted by Leadership IQ, a research and consulting firm, implies that we are often not adequately prepared for these conversations. It suggests that when managers criticize poor performance, they don't necessarily provide enough useful information to help correct the problem. Conversely, when managers praise excellent performance, their feedback does not always provide enough useful information to help performers repeat it.[3]

Giving feedback is not a natural skill for many of us, and consequently, it is often avoided. However, it's a critical element in the performance process, so it is important that we hone these skills and raise our comfort level.

Before moving on to the second Leader element, Operational Improvement, I'd like to note two concepts that impact effectiveness when conducting the performance conversations: 1) the distinction between leadership and management, and 2) the concept of the self-fulfilling prophecy.

Leadership vs. Management

The Leader role in the Triangle combines both leadership and management behaviors. Basically, leadership is seen as functioning on a

3. Mark Murphy, "Employees Are Desperate for Feedback," SuccessFactors Blog, October 29, 2009, http://www.successfactors.com/blogs/business-execution/performancereview/.

strategic level, challenging and inspiring people to reach their potential and achieve business targets. Whereas management is perceived as an operational function, ensuring that work is organized, complete, and done on time. When performance conversations are done well, those in the Leader role demonstrate both leadership and management characteristics. They have an ability to use language that engages and encourages performers, while also discussing operational details.

Our sense of what it means to be a leader can sometimes get in the way of making the right decision, especially when managers take pride in leading through knowing the best way to do things. This issue came up during an off-site planning session led by John, a Vice President of Operations for a national car rental company. At the beginning of the session, which included John's regional managers and their direct reports, the group had agreed upon a series of goals and listed a number of action items. When they were about to start narrowing down the list to the most worthy suggestions, John took me aside and said, "A number of my thoughts are on this list. How do I decide whose ideas to use?" I suggested a basic guideline: *As long as their ideas will achieve the same results as yours, by default, their ideas are better.*

Choosing the most effective actions is a judgment call, but the benefits gained by using the suggestions of those who report to you go a long way to establishing an ownership culture. It demonstrates both leadership and management decision-making. You show that you recognize their capability and value their opinions while also maintaining a focus on results.

The Self-Fulfilling Prophecy

Your success as a manager relies heavily on how well you conduct performance conversations. The way you treat people, based on what you think about their capabilities, makes a difference in how they perform. This theory comes from the phenomenon of the self-fulfilling prophecy, also known as the Pygmalion effect.

The concept is based on a Greek myth about Pygmalion, the king of Cyprus, who carved an ivory statue of his ideal woman. He was so enamored by the beauty of his creation that he fell in love with her and asked Aphrodite, the goddess of love, to bring her to life; which, as legend has it, she did.

We study myths to uncover meanings that we can apply to our world. Our interpretation of this story is that the statue came to life because of Pygmalion's great love and, more importantly, through his belief in Aphrodite's powers. Today, the story is used to underscore the concept of the self-fulfilling prophecy: that something will happen because of your beliefs and expectations.

A number of studies have been conducted to illustrate this power of expectations and beliefs. They involved telling teachers that certain students in their classes had higher intelligence scores than others, when in fact these students were selected at random. By the end of the measurement periods, it was found that the selected students did better on tests and were considered by fellow students to be among the most capable.[4]

Another study, this one conducted in the workplace, involved a business that produced medical kits. For years, the head supervisor had little confidence in the performance abilities of employees hired to be kit assemblers. For the study, he was told that a new group of hires had especially high performance potential, although these employees were no different than the previous ones. Based on this information, the supervisor expected the new group to achieve more and, in fact, it did surpass record production levels.[5]

---

4. Robert Rosenthal and Lenore Jacobson, *Pygmalion in the Classroom*, Norwalk, CT: Crown House Publishing, 1992.
5. Nicole M. Kierein and Michael A. Gold, "Pygmalion in work organizations: a meta-analysis," *Organization Behavior* 21, no. 8, John Wiley & Sons, Ltd., (December 2000): 913–928.

The lessons drawn from these studies suggest that people have a tendency to perform according to expectations, or the preconceived notions that others have of them. Although the teachers and supervisor were not aware of behaving in a special way toward those students or employees designated as high performers, it is hypothesized that through unconscious behavior, they treated them differently. They may have called on them more often, given them more challenging and stimulating assignments, or simply paid more attention to them because of their "potential." This treatment had profoundly affected how those thought to have high potential behaved and how they felt about themselves.

How you feel about someone, what you say, and how you say it can have a significant impact. Just as positive reinforcement can lead a performer to do well, negative comments could be detrimental. Those in the Leader role need to consider this phenomenon, because it is important to think about the message you intend to send and the consequences it will have on your results.

OPERATIONAL IMPROVEMENTS

The process of making operational improvements, the second element of the Leader role, highlights the need to constantly analyze and refine the way work is done. It requires regularly assessing the policies and procedures that have become ingrained in the organization's ways of doing business, as well as the impact that the organization's structure, culture, and politics have on its performance.

A case in which policies and procedures contributed to underperformance involved Lee, a purchasing manager for an international financial institution. He often received criticism for the amount of time it took to order and deliver office equipment. The problem was that many purchases required five executive signatures. If one of these executives was out of the office or not responding, the requisition languished. No one had considered the possibility that the number of signatures may have been excessive and contributed to a less efficient work process. The long-standing procedures kept Lee labeled as an underperformer. Once the issue became clear, management had a choice to adjust their expectations or change the procedure.

Another example is from my work with an international travel agency. In the U.S. reservations offices at that time, agents who worked on comission provided customers with travel vouchers that they would exchange for services along their trip. There were domestic vouchers for United States travel and international vouchers for trips outside of the U.S.

Management discovered that agents were giving domestic vouchers to all clients, even those traveling internationally. It turned out that the wrong vouchers were issued because the U.S. agents who arranged the booking were not getting the commission when international vouchers were used. Instead, the financial reward went to the agents in the country in which the voucher was redeemed. If management wanted the correct form employed, the reward policy needed adjustment so that the domestic agents received the commissions they were due.

Leaders have a responsibility to identify when existing policies and procedures are detrimental to the organization, and do what they can to change the way the company functions.

PULLING IT ALL TOGETHER

People who take on the Leader role are responsible for conducting performance conversations and making decisions to improve the organization's operational effectiveness. It is a complex role requiring a close working relationship with performers. Your level of success is determined by your ability to communicate in a way that engages people and maintains the focus on achieving goals. From this position, leaders can model the values and behaviors that they want to instill in the organization.

THE PERFORMER'S ROLE

The Triangle defines performers as those who perform the day-to-day tasks that move a business forward. They are usually thought of as being frontline employees. In fact, everyone in the organization takes on the performer role at one point or another.

If you are a manager, you're in the leader position in relation to those who report to you. However, you switch to the performer role many times throughout a day, such as when executing routine managerial tasks like budgeting or planning. When conducting performance conversations you are simultaneously functioning in both a leader and performer capacity. Even CEOs function as performers when they're carrying out duties like making presentations to the board of directors or conducting town hall meetings.

Effective performers routinely exhibit certain qualities. They are the right fit for the position, interested in the work, and able to manage time and priorities. The right fit suggests that performers have, or are able to obtain, the skills, knowledge, and experience to do the work, and possess the intellectual, psychological, and physical capacity to fill the role.

As it happens, it is not uncommon that people take jobs for reasons other than the 'right fit' or interest in the work: a good commute, friends in the organization, or simply the need of a paycheck. All are valid reasons, but in any case, you need to make an effort to understand management's expectations and do what's necessary to complete assignments successfully.

The focus of this chapter is on strategies for being effective in the role of performer. It suggests that regardless of whether you are a manager or frontline employee, in the performer position you must openly participate in performance conversations and develop an active-learning mindset.

PERFORMANCE CONVERSATIONS: THE PERFORMER'S PERSPECTIVE

The previous chapter examined the performance conversations from the leader's perspective. This chapter views them from the point of view of the performer.

The Expectations Conversation

When a task is delegated, it's important to understand the goals and expectations. Based on your experience and position in the organization, you may be able to provide insight and contribute ideas for implementing the assignment. If so, take the opportunity to show initiative and offer your thoughts. Conversely, if you feel uncertain about the assignment, ask for clarity. If you question your ability to manage it, be open about your concern. The objective of the conversation is to determine whether you are ready to take on the assignment. Once that has been determined, you can choose to take one of the following actions.

Accept   Ideally, accepting an assignment means you have a clear understanding of the goals and what is expected. Accepting suggests that you are ready to do what it takes to achieve the desired outcome, and to be accountable for the results.

Negotiate   If you're uncertain that you can complete the assignment as requested, think about negotiating before accepting. Offer a different approach, or suggest pushing back delivery times to be more realistic. If the decision goes against you, you have the choice to accept or refuse the work.

Refuse   To many, refusal is not a viable option. However, it *is* an option, although it comes with possible repercussions, like no longer being offered interesting or challenging assignments or even being let go. Refusal requires serious thought.

The purpose of the expectations conversation is to have a full, open discussion so you are informed about an assignment and prepared to be accountable. Even if your position allows you to delegate the work to others, you still carry the responsibility of its outcome. When you hand it off, you are not relinquished of that responsibility; it is now shared.

The Support Conversation

Support conversations are opportunities to report on progress: to discuss the work, raise concerns, and reaffirm or adjust schedules. As the performer, your objectives are to hear your manager's perceptions of the work so far, hash out any performance issues, and agree on plans for continuing.

Support meetings are not limited to discussing immediate assignments; they may also be scheduled to discuss general performance issues. As an example, a few years ago I coached Nadine, a manager who was feeling stress because of the pull between the growing demands of her job and the time she wanted to spend with her children. As a result, she shied away from taking on new assignments. Her boss had mentioned his concern that she was no longer up to the demands of her position.

We discussed a potential option to reduce her anxiety. It required making a request of her manager. In their next meeting, Nadine asked to work out of the office one day a week so she could be around when her children left for school and came home in the afternoon.

Her manager accepted the idea. When I saw Nadine about a month later, she was more relaxed even while taking on more challenges in the office. Though it may not always be possible for your manager to accommodate your requests, if you need additional support to be more effective in your role, it's worthwhile to ask.

The Feedback Conversation

Receiving feedback is a critical aspect of the performance process. Positive feedback is always welcomed; however, in the same way that many managers are uncomfortable giving corrective feedback, many of us are fearful about receiving it and become defensive.

When getting feedback, it behooves you to be open to what you hear and participate in the conversation. Even though we all want to receive praise, corrective observations are learning opportunities that bring attention to behaviors that need to change.

Hearing how your work is being perceived is an integral part of becoming a high performer. If you are not receiving feedback, it's worthwhile to seek it out. Whether positive or corrective, it provides information that can help you further your personal development, correct any misperceptions, and assess if you are a good fit for your position.

ACTIVE LEARNING

Having accepted a task, it's up to performers to be as effective and efficient as possible. If the work is not progressing well, a change is necessary. The active-learning process provides a technique for boosting your level of performance. It involves incorporating a three-phase work discipline: 1) take an action, 2) assess the results, and 3) adjust behavior.

The objective is to increase effectiveness by recognizing which actions add value and which waste time, and then doing everything possible to eliminate the waste. Each time you cycle through this learning process, you have additional opportunities to assess your efforts and raise performance levels.

Although streamlining workflow is the main method for improving efficiency, the following case presents the improvement process in a broader perspective. Rob, a manager in the IT department of an investment bank, had developed a dysfunctional work habit. He had a tendency to help others to the detriment of taking care of his own duties. Therefore, although he was highly skilled in his area of expertise, he continually fell behind in his work.

Action   Because Rob was an expert in his subject, colleagues came to him for assistance in completing their projects. He spent a good deal of time during the workday assisting others.

Results   It became clear that people expected Rob to be available. As a result, he often had to stay late to catch up on his own assignments. His desire to assist others added unnecessary amounts of pressure and became detrimental to the quality of his own work.

Adjust   Through discussing the situation, Rob realized that he could not continue this behavior. He needed to reset expectations.

Action   He set aside specific hours when he would be available and informed his co-workers.

Results   His own projects were completed without having to stay late, and he found himself more focused when others asked for his attention.

Often we find ourselves in situations that need to change, yet we don't take the time to consider and fix. The active-learning mindset is an invaluable discipline. It can lead to the development of more effective work processes, and engage us in the challenge of raising our performance to the highest levels.

PULLING IT ALL TOGETHER

Although leaders set direction, provide support, and give feedback, it is the performer who is responsible for full participation in performance conversations and doing the work that moves an organization forward. This partnership is critical for executing plans and achieving the organization's goals. In order to be truly effective, performers need to develop an active-learning mindset and a discipline for fine-tuning the work process.

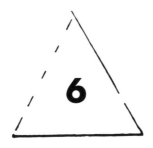

THE TASKS

Tasks represent the work that takes place within an organization. This chapter defines the three components that make up the Triangle's task element: workflow, obstacles, and consequences. Each is critical to the performance process, and consequently must be taken into consideration when leaders and performers discuss implementation plans.

TASK COMPONENTS

Workflow

Workflow is similar to walking: putting one foot in front of the other to get to where you want to go. You can improve efficiency and effectiveness in getting from point A to point B by changing your stride, adjusting your posture, or wearing the right kind of shoes. When doing tasks in the workplace, we essentially take one step at a time.

The responsibility of leaders and performers is to weed out wasted motion. This can be achieved by eliminating unnecessary steps and fine-tuning those that are more complicated than they need to be. No matter how skilled and dedicated people are, they cannot be at their best when working within flawed processes.

I saw an example of efficient workflow on a recent business trip to Chicago. I was having dinner at the bar of a busy restaurant and noticed that when servers came to pick up drinks, they would also return used glasses, putting them onto a conveyor belt. This transported the glasses to the dishwasher, who then placed them back onto the conveyor belt to be returned to the bar area. During his routine of taking orders and making drinks, the bartender would reach over to the clean glasses and place them back into their proper slots. In most restaurants, busboys struggle in the limited space behind the bar to return the clean glassware. Here the process was quick, simple, and neat.

By streamlining tasks and removing obstacles, high-performing organizations constantly strive toward this sort of efficiency. Improving workflow is a vast topic. From the *total quality management* concepts that have evolved into the *lean management* practices used today, there is a plethora of information on the subject of streamlining work so that it is efficient, cost-effective, and focused on quality.

Obstacles

Obstacles to getting work done are found in outdated policies, procedures, and equipment; poorly considered use of office space; or inadequate staffing. Ideally, performance inhibitors such as these are identified when action plans are initially devised. Unfortunately, these kinds of obstacles are often imbedded in organizational routines and require well-thought-out strategies to remove or change them.

A good example of this is the case of Rick, an operations manager for a printing plant. His job was in jeopardy because he wasn't responding to problems as quickly as Steven, the CEO, expected. When Steven established the company, he took an office overlooking the shop floor so he could readily observe what was going on. He subsequently hired

Rick and gave him the responsibility of overseeing the operations.

Steven requested a meeting with Rick to discuss the situation, at which time it was determined that because Rick's office was down the hall, he couldn't see the shop floor from his desk. When it became apparent that this was the issue, they switched offices, and the performance problem dissolved.

In hindsight, this seems like an obvious way to resolve the problem, but since Steven and Rick were operating as they always had, they'd been unable to see the simple solution. Similarly, in the example of Lee, the purchasing manager, the five signatures required on requisitions clearly interfered with his ability to perform efficiently. In many organizations, these kinds of obstacles are tolerated and overlooked.

Consequences

In the course of doing work, performers can experience both positive and negative consequences. For instance, when I'm having problems with my computer and call technical support, I'm usually exhibiting a high level of frustration. If I receive patient help and the issue is resolved, I will let the support person know that I'm appreciative of the assistance. In this way, I'm providing a positive consequence to the person who helped me.

However, even though the support representative provided effective help, if the time it took to resolve the problem required him to stay late, causing him to miss his train, that would be a negative consequence for him. If this is a common occurrence for workers in this role, the effect could be demoralizing and have an impact on their performance.

When planning tasks, you want to be conscious of the effects that both positive and negative consequences can have, and attempt to build in opportunities for people to have positive experiences while removing the causes of negative ones. When negative consequences cannot be avoided, performers need to be trained to keep them in perspective. Without that preparation, jobs that produce negative experiences can quickly become stressful and discourage enthusiastic workers.

TASKS AS MOTIVATORS

The degree to which people are able to complete tasks effectively and efficiently affects their attitudes just as much as it determines an organization's level of success. We spend a lot of time looking for work efficiencies, but often lose sight of how the work process affects performer motivation.

In the 1950s and '60s, Fredrick Herzberg conducted landmark research about what motivated people in the workplace. His research suggests that people are essentially motivated by five factors: achievement, recognition, the work itself, advancement, and growth.

Around the time that Herzberg was doing his research, an embryonic movement called 'job enrichment' started introducing motivational elements into the work process. Herzberg used his motivational factors to contribute to the new field by introducing the principles known as 'vertical job loading.'[6] Examples of his contribution include:

▲ *Removing controls from a task while retaining accountability.*
This encourages the performer to take *responsibility* for the results of the work and provides a sense of personal a*chievement.*

▲ *Introducing new and more difficult tasks not previously handled.*
This promotes opportunities for *learning* and *growth.*

▲ *Assigning individuals specific or specialized tasks.*
This provides appropriate challenges and shows that management recognizes when one is ready for additional *responsibility* and is prepared to *grow.*

6. Frederick Herzberg, "One More Time, How Do You Motivate Employees?" *Harvard Business Review*, Reprint #87507, (September–October 1987): 10–13.

The concepts of vertical job loading and job enrichment are more about how to design work than how to treat workers themselves. The objective is to create a work environment that recognizes the personal contributions of performers and provides opportunities for growth.

PULLING IT ALL TOGETHER

This chapter described the three components for improving task effectiveness: workflow, obstacles, and consequences. The degree to which organizations succeed is determined by the amount of attention given to these elements. The objective is to design tasks that engage performers and allow them to complete their work with the minimum of interference. It's crucial to an effective performance process that leaders and performers take the time to consider each component when discussing assignments and planning how to best implement tasks.

7

A SUMMING UP

In the introduction to this book, I wrote that lessons learned from the research on employee engagement and high-performance literature offer insights for developing an execution-focused workplace. These lessons suggest that employees become engaged and perform better when they:

▲ Have *open, trusting relationships* with their managers

▲ Are *appropriately challenged* by day-to-day work and are *given opportunities for growth*

▲ Have *clear targets* that are *valued as contributing* toward achieving business goals

▲ Feel that their *opinions count* and are *taken into consideration* in decision making

▲ Receive *regular feedback* on their performance and are *recognized for successes*

By implementing all elements of the Triangle, organizations can create a workplace culture in which the above characteristics are incorporated. However, it is the following three strategies that represent the core disciplines of the Triangle: 1) conducting performance conversations, 2) maintaining an action-learning mindset, and 3) creating an ongoing improvement process. In order to embed these strategies into your operations, senior management needs to regularly emphasize and reinforce their use.

THE CORE DISCIPLINES

Conduct Performance Conversations

The performance conversations provide a foundation for creating open, trusting relationships between leaders and performers. Through this framework, performers have opportunities to share their knowledge and opinions, as well as advocate for their point of view. Leaders who learn to effectively conduct these discussions and adopt ideas suggested by others can create a culture in which personal accountability becomes the norm.

This strategy is the linchpin of the Triangle. Organizations, even those with robust, on-the-mark business strategies, will largely succeed or fail because of the relationships and communications that exist between their leaders and performers.

Maintain an Active-Learning Mindset

An active-learning mindset is a critical discipline to develop if an organization hopes to increase its proficiency and productivity. It is a self-generated learning process that pushes performers toward continually challenging themselves, as well as the organization for which they work. Ideally, performers learn to maintain a conscious focus on goals and seek the most effective path. This mindset must be nurtured and celebrated for it to become an integral part of an organization's operational culture.

Create an Ongoing Improvement Process

Ongoing process improvement involves routinely reviewing and streamlining how work is done throughout an organization. Whereas the goal of an active-learning mindset is short-term and immediate learning, process improvement often requires a longer-term view and the courage to make the necessary changes.

Leaders and performers are partners in this endeavor. Performers, who are closer to the day-to-day operational realities, are in position to observe and recommend areas for improvement. Leaders are in position to make decisions required to initiate operational changes. Their combined efforts drive the performance improvement process.

The Triangle elements, and particularly these three strategies, require diligent attention for them to become pervasive throughout your organization. They provide the framework for creating an engaged workforce, one motivated to do what it takes to reach its goals.

THE TRIANGLE AS A MOTIVATIONAL STRATEGY

Motivation is one of those recurring management and leadership topics. We keep searching for some magical set of rewards and recognition programs that will motivate the diverse group of people who work in our organizations.

Many of us have had success igniting a spark now and then. We've witnessed energy spurts and good feelings after well-planned team activities that bring people together. We've seen frontline workers invigorated after their ideas were used to successfully solve a sticky operational problem. A bonus or a raise is always welcome, especially when it's seen as recognition for hard work and accomplishments. These kinds of actions can produce a transitory boost in a group's enthusiasm and, if we're lucky, improve performance for a while. However, it is a focus on individuals and our ability to respond to their needs and goals that will provide the real, lasting leverage for success.

This requires caring about those who work for us and with us, and doing what we can to make time spent in the workplace a fulfilling experience. Wherever performer needs and interests can be taken into account, the organization should strive to do so—if employees are engaged and satisfied, everyone benefits.

The final word goes to William McKnight, Chairman of 3M from 1949 to 1966. He championed the leadership and management practices encapsulated in the Triangle Strategy when he noted that as businesses grow ". . . it becomes increasingly necessary to delegate responsibility and to encourage men and women to exercise their initiative." He recognized that ". . . mistakes will be made. But if a person is essentially right, the mistakes he or she makes are not as serious in the long run as the mistakes management will make if it undertakes to tell those under its authority exactly how they must do their jobs."[7]

As mentioned at the outset, the Triangle Strategy does not espouse new theories but reminds us of the wisdom and best practices that have been with us for decades. We simply need to pay attention.

---

7. William McKnight, from McKnight Principles, http://solutions.3m.com/wps/portal/3M/en_WW/History/3M/Company/McKnight-principles/

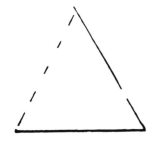

APPENDIX

APPLYING THE TRIANGLE

The purpose of this section is to provide a few examples of how to apply the Triangle in your work. I've chosen four situations that are commonly found in the workplace and honed them down to their essentials. I suggest that you start with the case that is most relevant and interesting to you. My hope is that by reading these cases, you will identify additional situations for using the Triangle in your organization and begin to see the disciplined thought process it leads you through. The situations include:

1. Delegating an assignment

2. Improving underperformance

3. Introducing a change initiative

4. Transitioning to a new management role

An instructional note: When using the Triangle as an analysis and planning tool, you should start by identifying 1) the goal, 2) the leader, 3) the performers, and 4) the task. Then you have a choice of creating an illustration of the Triangle, which will provide a quick snapshot of the situation, or writing a more detailed description using the Triangle elements as an outline. Depending on your needs, either method will help you organize your thoughts.

DELEGATING AN ASSIGNMENT

Delegating work to others is a normal management task. Because of its routine nature, managers often do not think through their expectations or other performance issues before handing off assignments. The following case provides an example of how a manager used the Triangle to plan for conducting the delegation meeting.

Situation: Jean manages the administrative functions in a nonprofit grant-making organization. She wanted to change their grant process to one that was paperless and planned to delegate the assignment to Tracy, whose job was to oversee the management of the grant records.

Go to the Triangle: First, Jean created an illustrated Triangle to quickly jot down her initial thoughts. Next, she used the Triangle outline to broaden her understanding of the assignment.

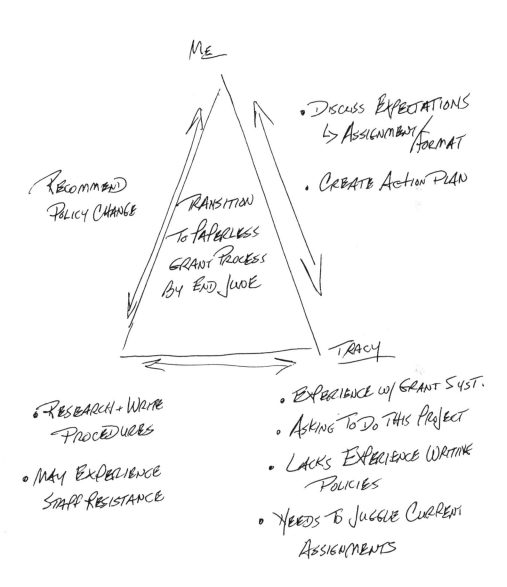

ME

- DISCUSS EXPECTATIONS
  ↳ ASSIGNMENT/FORMAT
- CREATE ACTION PLAN

RECOMMEND
POLICY CHANGE

TRANSITION
TO PAPERLESS
GRANT PROCESS
BY END JUNE

TRACY

- EXPERIENCE W/ GRANT SYST.
- ASKING TO DO THIS PROJECT
- LACKS EXPERIENCE WRITING
  POLICIES
- NEEDS TO JUGGLE CURRENT
  ASSIGNMENTS

- RESEARCH + WRITE
  PROCEDURES
- MAY EXPERIENCE
  STAFF RESISTANCE

The illustration provides a visual representation of some of the issues involved. An outline, such as the one Jean made below, is a more comprehensive analysis.

Goals   *Purpose:* Develop a policy that provides guidance to the staff on how to maintain electronic grant records.

Target: Test and implement the new policy by the end of June.

Balance: Make sure the procedure is accurate, clear, and easy to use.

Leaders   *Set Expectations:* Although Tracy has experience administering the grant records, I'll have to be very clear about the need to make the new procedures user-friendly.

Provide Support: Schedule regular meetings to review her progress and assess her needs.

Give Feedback: Highlight areas where she's being effective and areas that need improvement.

Operational Improvement: Recommend the change in policy to the executive team.

Performers   *Fit:* Tracy has been maintaining both electronic and paper records for two years, so she understands the issues involved in transitioning to a paperless office. However, she does not have experience writing policies.

Interest: She has wanted to reduce our reliance on paper for a while and has asked to be involved with this change.

Self-Management: Although Tracy is self-directed and is able to juggle multiple tasks well, she will need to do this project along with her normal daily tasks. Time management may be an issue, so I will need to monitor that her workload remains manageable.

Tasks

Workflow: Before drafting the new policy, Tracy will need to research other foundations that have made similar transitions to learn how they instituted their policies and procedures.

Obstacles: There is a chance that the staff will be resistant to making this change. It will require them to upload documents directly to our database rather than dropping a hard copy on Tracy's desk for filing. I will encourage Tracy to meet with staff members to understand their concerns and take them into consideration when developing the new policy.

Consequences: It's possible that resistance to new procedures could make this a negative experience for Tracy. Hopefully, by reaching out to others as she moves forward, this will not be an issue. I will need to monitor this aspect of the project and possibly be involved in some of these conversations.

From her analysis, Jean realized that she needed to spend time with Tracy to make sure that she was both comfortable with taking on the project and understood what was required. Jean also identified that it would be important to engage other staff members during the process of developing and implementing the new policy.

IMPROVING UNDERPERFORMANCE

A manager's challenge is to develop and maintain a high-performance work team. Frequently, and despite best efforts, work can veer off track. Below is a scenario that demonstrates how to use the Triangle to resolve a situation in which underperformance has become an issue.

Situation: Tina heads up a customer service center for a manufacturing company. Part of the organization consists of teams assigned to fielding calls for different products. One of her teams has been mentioned in the monthly report for not using correct procedures to resolve client issues on several occasions. Tina realizes that she's been distracted with other priorities and has not paid sufficient attention to this team. She plans to meet with her team to try to figure out how to improve the situation.

Go to the Triangle: By using the Triangle, Tina is able to identify the issues that need to be discussed.

Goals	*Purpose:* Reinforce the value of the work that the team does.
	Target/Balance: Review how the team's performance is being measured.
Leaders	*Give Feedback:* Discuss the error report.
	Provide Support: Ask for the team's reaction to the situation.
	Set Expectations: Reestablish my expectations for the team.
Performers	*Fit/Self-Management:* Assesses the team's ability to field the calls; determine whether more training would be useful.
	Interest: Assess their level of interest in working in this department.

Tasks	*Workflow:* Evaluate the procedures for answering these calls.
	Obstacles/Consequences: Investigate if there are obstructions or distractions affecting their results.

The Triangle provides a general set of topics that can be used to investigate any situation in which underperformance is an issue. They help to quickly identify the areas that impact performance levels and offer a vehicle for engaging performers in this conversation.

INTRODUCING A CHANGE INITIATIVE

Change initiatives are a constant in organizations, whether in the form of new technology, policies, procedures, or ways of organizing the business. Although varying in complexity, all successful change projects have certain elements in common. They require clear goals, leaders who understand their roles, and performers who are able to execute tasks according to plan.

This case highlights how these elements come into play when changing a healthcare policy.

Situation: Peter, the CEO of a software development company, felt that costs for their healthcare benefits plan were getting too high. He asked Barbara, the VP of Human Resources, to investigate other options. Barbara assigned the project to Nicole, who did the research and presented her recommendation to Barbara and Peter. After further discussions with the new insurance vendor, a final set of options was chosen. Nicole was then assigned to implement the change.

Go to the Triangle: In order to clarify what needed to be done, Nicole used the Triangle to construct a plan.

Goals	*Purpose:* To provide the best possible benefits program to employees while staying in line with the company's cost structure.
	Target: Have everyone enrolled in the new healthcare package by the third quarter.
	Balance: Although we need to implement this change quickly, we want to allow enough time to answer all employee concerns.
Leaders	*Set Expectations:* We need to be clear that the company remains committed to providing effective coverage. We'll continue monitoring the program to ensure it includes appropriate new options as they are introduced by the insurance industry.
	Provide Support: Representatives from the insurance company will present the new plan and be available to answer any questions. They will also offer a hotline that can be called after the plan has been implemented.
	Give Feedback: I need to communicate to employees that we will keep them informed of our progress as we lower our costs.
Performers	*Fit:* This change will impact everyone employed by the company. It is important that we provide enough information so people understand the new options.
	Interest: The current plan is well liked. Employees will want to know how this change will affect them personally.
	Self-Management: We are allowing a month for people to discuss the changes and make decisions with their families. It is up to them to elect the new policies before the deadline.

Tasks   *Workflow:* After sending out information packets regarding the new plan, I will conduct Q&A sessions with the staff. Employees can then select and sign up for the plan that best fits their needs.

Obstacles: If we conduct our Q&A meetings effectively and provide an easy registration process, there shouldn't be any obstacles.

Consequences: The way I present the plan will determine whether the feedback from the staff is positive or negative.

By conducting this analysis, Nicole realized that she would need Peter and Barbara to make statements about their commitment to continue offering a high level of health insurance. She also knew that she needed to figure out the best way to conduct the Q&A sessions and provide time for further questions after people had discussed the changes with their families.

This case describes a fairly straightforward change project. An initiative involving a broader organizational change would require identifying the issues and needs at different levels of the organization. A cascading set of illustrated Triangles can be useful for this purpose. The following example demonstrates how this hierarchal approach works.

TRANSITIONING TO A NEW MANAGEMENT ROLE

The transition of moving into a new management role can take a number of different forms. It could be a promotion from a frontline position to a supervisory or managerial assignment, or it could involve a manager being transferred to lead a different group. Whether you are a frontline employee or an experienced manager, many aspects of moving into new roles are similar. Following is the case with Lisa, who was recently promoted to a management role.

Situation: Lisa has been working as a fabric designer in her company for seven years. Daniel, her manager, was recently promoted and wants Lisa to take over their group. She is interested in the challenge, but is not sure how to go about making the transition.

Go to the Triangle: In the process of doing her analysis, Lisa realized that before she would be ready to move into the management position, she needed to discuss the role with Daniel. The second step would be to meet with her team. Therefore, she drew two Triangles. The first depicts Lisa as the Performer, with Daniel in the Leader role. In the second, she is in the Leader position, as well as in the Performer position along with the members of her team.

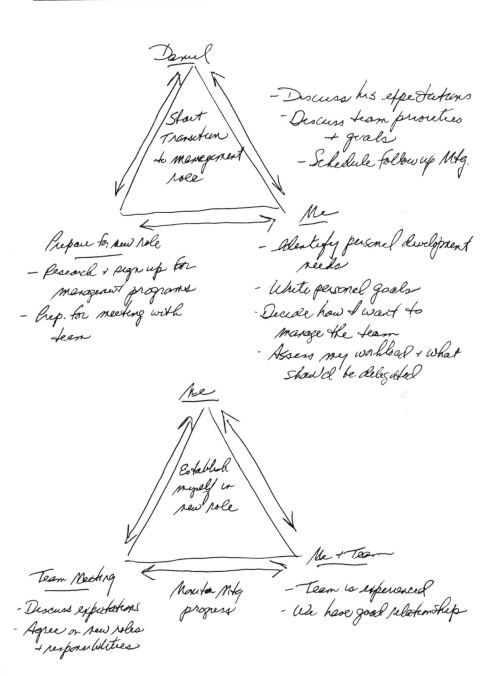

Daniel

Start Transition to management role

- Discuss his expectations
- Discuss team priorities + goals
- Schedule follow up Mtg.

Me

Prepare for new role
- Research + sign up for management programs
- Prep. for meeting with team

- Identify personal development needs
- Write personal goals
- Decide how I want to manage the team
- Assess my workload + what should be delegated

Me

Establish myself in new role

Me + Team

Team Meeting
- Discuss expectations
- Agree on new roles + responsibilities

Monitor Mtg progress

- Team is experienced
- We have good relationship

65

As a designer, Lisa is a visual person; therefore, drawing the two Triangles was sufficient for her. They provided a graphic snapshot of discussions she needed to have with Daniel and her team.

PULLING IT ALL TOGETHER

The elements of the Triangle Strategy provide leads for your thought process. When working with either the Triangle illustration or outline approach, the trick is to not get stuck if an idea does not fit neatly into one of the categories. Instead, write it down. As you continue, you will either find a place for the idea, or you may recognize that it does not help advance your analysis and you will discard it. With either approach, the aim is to gain a broad understanding of the performance issues at hand and develop comprehensive execution plans. The only way to truly understand how the Triangle works is to try it out.

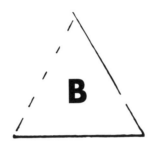

WRITING GOALS

The first phase in the performance process is to identify well-defined goals. The Triangle suggests using a framework that includes three components: purpose, target, and balance. Following is a four-step excercise to guide you through the activity of writing goals that are complete and easily communicated.

Step 1: Identify the Situation
What is a general description of the work to be done?

Step 2: Clarify the Purpose
If the assignment is completed successfully, what is the benefit to you, your team, your organization, and/or your community?

Step 3: Define the Target
What is the desired result and time frame for achieving that result?

Step 4: Establish a Balance
How will you measure success?

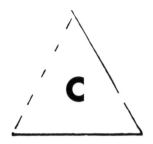

LEVEL-SETTING EXPECTATIONS (LSE)

It is as important to establish a baseline of mutual understanding at the beginning of a working relationship as it is when delegating an assignment. The Level-Setting Expectations (LSE) exercise helps leaders and performers jump-start new relationships and establish guidelines for working together.

Following is a three-step approach to conducting the exercise.

Step 1: Create LSE Charts

The manager and direct report(s) each create a T-chart, as illustrated below.

I expect from you	You can expect from me

Step 2: Fill Out the Charts

Before filling out the charts, allow some time for people to think about their expectations. Below are examples of a few items that may appear on these charts.

Manager's Chart

I expect from you	You can expect from me
Be at work on time	Be open to new ideas
Participate in meetings	Be available to answer questions
Point out potential problems	Be considerate of work pressures

Direct Report's Chart

I expect from you	You can expect from me
Give feedback about the quality of my work	Think of ways to improve my effectiveness
Be available for questions	Be diligent in my work
Follow through on decisions	Respond to feedback

Step 3: Discuss the Charts

Once the charts are complete, the parties meet and compare notes. In a sense, the discussion becomes an unofficial negotiation process and forms a foundation for working together. Although the success of these meetings relies on an open, give-and-take discussion, it remains the manager's prerogative to make final decisions. Initially, the manager may not want or be able to do everything requested by the subordinate, and vice versa. These are important items for discussion and clarification.

GENERAL NOTES ABOUT THE LSE PROCESS

There are a number of issues to consider when using the LSE process.

1. The process is meant to start the conversation. Just because ideas are in writing does not mean they are set in stone. The lists may change over time and with experience.

2. There will be situations in which employees who are new to a team may also be new to the workforce, and therefore might not have much to contribute at first. In these situations, managers can encourage them to contribute by explaining the intention of the exercise.

3. It's possible that more experienced workers can have a fruitful discussion without the writing step. The goal is that by the end of the discussion, there is a clear understanding of how to proceed.

4. The process forces leaders to identify the values and behaviors they want to incorporate into their management approach.

THE PERFORMANCE SCAN

One objective of leaders is to develop teams of high performers. The Performance Scan provides managers with a framework to help them identify the amount of attention needed by each member of their team in order to build and maintain a sufficiently high level of performance. It is an exercise that suggests managers examine the productivity of their direct reports through the criteria of job performance and job satisfaction.

Job Performance refers to the level of execution a person brings to the organization.

Job Satisfaction refers to the level of well-being a person feels within the organization.

The following chart can be used to do a performance scan. It is built around two axes: one signifies high and low levels of *performance*; the other signifies high and low levels of *satisfaction*. The two axes form four quadrants.

High Performance

H/L High performers who are less satisfied with the job	**H/H** High performers who receive personal satisfaction from the job
L/L Low performers who are dissatisfied with the job	**L/H** Low performers who enjoy the job

Low Satisfaction (left) — **High Satisfaction** (right)

Low Performance

To use the chart, identify where you feel each member of your team would fall, thinking of each quadrant as though it were a grid. For instance, in Quadrant H/H, place your highest and most satisfied performers in the upper-right corner. Those who you feel are less productive but still highly satisfied would be placed lower and toward the left side of that quadrant. At the other extreme, those who are performing badly and you think don't really like the work would be placed near the lower-left corner in Quadrant L/L.

An example of a scan of a team of eight people is shown below.

High Performance

Julia	Sara
	Anna
Pete	Jim

Low Satisfaction | **High Satisfaction**

	David
Carl	
	Emma

Low Performance

Sara is the best performer and is very satisfied.

Jim is highly satisfied and is performing well.

Anna is a high-level performer, but her satisfaction level seems to be waning.

Julia is a high-level performer, but she is showing increased dissatisfaction.

Pete has become dissatisfied, although his performance is still acceptable.

David is highly satisfied, but his performance level is below expectations.

Emma is fairly satisfied, but her performance has become a real concern.

Carl is underperforming and clearly does not enjoy the work.

The performance scan is a subjective exercise that provides a quick snapshot of individual levels of satisfaction and performance. Once you've identified where team members fall in each of the quadrants, the next step is to figure out how to move them in the direction of Quadrant H/H. Once you've made this initial assessment, it's important to meet with each performer to share your perceptions, discuss the situation, and make appropriate plans.

Following are brief descriptions of performers who fall into each quadrant and strategies for working with them.

High/High   *Description:* Performers who are the right fit for their role and achieve performance goals. They are interested and find satisfaction in their work, and are ready for additional challenges.

Strategy: Acknowledge their accomplishments, and discuss opportunities for continued development that would help them grow in their areas of interest.

High/Low   *Description:* Performers who are effective in their role but seem to have lost interest or have simply become dissatisfied with some aspects of the work. Unless the situation is addressed, these people may continue to lose their motivation and eventually leave.

Strategy: Acknowledge their level of performance, and raise the issue that they seem to have lost interest in the work. Let them know that you are concerned, and ask what can be done to change the situation.

Low/High   *Description:* Performers whose performance results are below expectations but enjoy working in the organization. They will most likely continue in this way if you let them.

                    Strategy: Provide corrective feedback and reset expectations. Discuss ideas for turning the situation around, but be clear about the consequences of continued poor performance.

Low/Low   *Description:* Performers who are the wrong fit for the role. They do not perform well or get personal satisfaction from the work. They are neither helping themselves nor the organization.

                    Strategy: Be clear that unless their performance improves, they will be let go. Present the idea that since their performance is poor and they don't seem to be enjoying their work, the organization may not be a good fit, and they should consider looking for a job that is more suited to their interests and talents.

PERFORMANCE CONVERSATION SURVEYS

The Triangle identifies performance conversations as one of its critical strategies for success. This section contains two surveys to help reinforce those discussions: one for leaders, the other for performers. These assessments pertain to how you conduct or participate in performance conversations. They are intended to be thought-provoking—to help you personalize information contained in the book.

The survey questions are behavioral-based, because your effectiveness in the leader or performer role is a product of what you do, not what you know. In responding to the questions, you will need to reflect on your actions as a leader or a performer when engaged in the performance conversations.

After answering the survey questions, you will find a format for writing down personal insights.

PERFORMANCE CONVERSATION SURVEY: THE LEADER'S POINT OF VIEW

The objective of this survey is to raise awareness of how to conduct performance conversations. The survey has been divided into three sections, each designated by the name of one of the conversations. Read each statement, and think about how often you practice that behavior. Then, using the following scale, write the point value of the rating in the designated column.

1 = Never
2 = Rarely
3 = Sometimes
4 = Most of the time
5 = Always

Expectation Conversations

When assigning a task to staff members . . .   Rating

	Rating
1. We discuss their ability to manage it along with their other priorities.	
2. I solicit ideas regarding the best way to achieve the goals.	
3. The benefits of achieving the goals are discussed.	
4. We talk about how the results will be measured.	
5. I am clear about my expectation that they take responsibility for completing the work.	
6. We discuss whether they require additional skills and/ or knowledge in order to complete it successfully.	
7. We consider potential obstacles.	

Support Conversations

When staff members are working on assignments . . .   Rating

8. I let them know that I'm available if they need assistance.	
9. I encourage suggestions for improving how the work can be done.	
10. I make sure to schedule times to review progress.	

Feedback Conversations

When giving positive feedback to staff members . . .   Rating

11. I am explicit about what was done well.	
12. I ask for ideas that could improve the work process.	

When giving corrective feedback to staff members . . .

13. I ask for their reactions.	
14. I encourage them to suggest solutions for improvement.	
15. I am clear about the behavior that I expect.	
16. After repeated corrective feedback meetings, I let them know their behavior is unacceptable and could lead to dismissal if performance is not improved.	

Assessing the Results: Each question has a potential rating of 5. Use your ratings to identify methods for improving how you conduct performance conversations. For instance, a rating of 3 or lower would suggest an area for development. The survey is meant to spur individual reflection. Following is space for writing down your thoughts.

Personal Insights
Review your survey responses. What thoughts do you have about areas in which you're doing well, or areas in which you could make improvements?

Expectation Conversations
Do Well/Could Do Better

_____
_____
_____
_____
_____
_____
_____
_____
_____

Support Conversations
Do Well/Could Do Better

_____
_____
_____
_____
_____
_____
_____
_____
_____

Feedback Conversations

Do Well/Could Do Better

PERFORMANCE CONVERSATION SURVEY: THE PERFORMER'S POINT OF VIEW

The objective of this survey is to raise awareness of how to participate in performance conversations. The survey has been divided into three sections, each designated by the name of one of the conversations. Read each statement, and think about how often you practice that behavior. Then, using the following scale, write the point value of the rating in the designated column.

1 = Never
2 = Rarely
3 = Sometimes
4 = Most of the time
5 = Always

Expectation Conversations

When accepting a task . . .

	Rating
1. I consider my ability to manage it along with my other responsibilities.	
2. I make sure the goals are clear to me.	
3. I seek to understand the benefits of achieving the goal.	
4. I feel comfortable asking for assistance if I require additional skills, knowledge, and/or support to be successful.	
5. I make sure to understand how the work will be measured.	
6. I take the responsibility of seeing the work through to completion seriously.	

	Rating
7. I contribute ideas about what I feel is the best way to achieve the goal.	
8. I try to identify and discuss potential obstacles that could interfere with reaching the task goal.	

Support Conversations

When I'm working on an assignment . . .	Rating
9. I am comfortable asking for assistance if needed.	
10. I schedule time with my manager to review and assess how the project is going.	
11. I see review meetings with my manager as learning opportunities.	

Feedback Conversations

When receiving positive feedback . . .	Rating
12. I seek to understand the behavior that is being praised so that I continue doing it.	
13. I offer ideas for improving the organization, if appropriate.	

When receiving corrective feedback . . .	
14. I try to listen without getting defensive.	
15. I make sure to understand what behavior is expected.	
16. I am comfortable sharing my point of view if I feel my performance is being assessed incorrectly.	
17. I suggest solutions for correcting the situation.	

Assessing the Results: Each question has a potential rating of 5. Use your ratings to identify methods for improving how you participate in performance conversations. For instance, a rating of 3 or lower would suggest an area for development. The survey is meant to spur individual reflection. Following is space for writing down your thoughts.

Personal Insights

Review your survey responses. What thoughts do you have about areas in which you're doing well, or areas in which you could make improvements?

Expectation Conversations

Do Well/Could Do Better

_____

_____

_____

_____

_____

_____

_____

Support Conversations

Do Well/Could Do Better

_____

_____

_____

_____

_____

_____

_____

Feedback Conversations

Do Well/Could Do Better

_____

_____

_____

_____

_____

_____

_____

_____

_____

_____

ACKNOWLEDGMENTS

I owe a major debt of gratitude to all of those who have led and contributed to the fields of performance management, and organization and leadership development. Their research, writings, and teachings have informed every aspect of this book as well as my work with students and clients. The book *Productive Workplaces* by Marvin Weisbord and the work of Gary Rummler and Robert Mager have framed my thoughts for many years.

I would like to take this opportunity to thank a number of people who have been supportive of this project. Marvin Gottlieb was an early supporter of the Triangle concepts and continues to be my friend and mentor. Through years of working together, Mitch Rosen and I have had many discussions about performance issues that helped to shape the concepts espoused in this book. Colleagues at Partners International have provided a sounding board and valuable insight as the Triangle developed. Dan White gave of his time to coach me through early stages of the work. John Hoover helped me make sense of the Triangle concepts in the earliest writings and has continued his support up to the present version. Additionally, Trish Kyle, Sean Harvey, Lisa Hennig, Cindy Levine, Peter Prichard, Steven Yorra, and Neil Eisenstein have provided thoughtful and useful feedback.

I owe special thanks to a few people who provided me with opportunities to work on projects in which the Triangle concepts were formed. Donna Marcus and Karen Hartman provided multiple occasions to be involved with international clients. Over a number of years, Frank Ribaudo brought my concepts to his organization's field managers through a series of training forums. These were invaluable opportunities.

Additionally, thank you David Harper, Paul Gorrell, Patrick Mulvey, and Paul Marciano, who all read early portions of the manuscript or discussed the Triangle with me and made helpful comments.

I am grateful to the New York University School of Continuing and Professional Studies department of Leadership and Human Capital Management for offering my program, Creating a High-Performance Workplace, in which the Triangle provides the foundation for learning. Thanks go to Roseanna DeMaria, who recognized the value of these concepts and introduced me to the university. My students have contributed greatly to this work through their challenges, insights, and applications of the concepts. Their stories and those of clients have provided examples throughout the book. For purposes of confidentiality, I have changed names and withheld details of their organizations.

This project has also been a family affair. Jamie Selzer, my copy editor, did much more than that position traditionally implies. Her keen editorial judgment and creative insights have been instrumental in finding the right form for the material. She has made the text coherent, accessible, and engaging. I could not have completed the book without her dedication and commitment.

Dan Selzer provided the book's design including the cover, layout, and internal graphics. His attention to detail, astute creativity, and understanding of the material have produced a look that gives a lift to the text and helps to make it an enjoyable read.

My wife, Carol Selzer, has provided support and encouragement from the beginning, reading and editing multiple versions of the manuscript. Her patience and insights throughout our many discussions about the Triangle helped me to remain focused and continually moving forward with this project.

ABOUT THE AUTHOR

Michael Tull has over twenty-five years of national and international experience as a consultant, coach, manager, and trainer in a wide range of industries. His commitment is to improving individual and workplace performance through client involvement.

Michael's consulting engagements span Fortune 500 companies in a broad range of industries, entrepreneurial businesses, and state and local government agencies. He earned a Masters of Education from Columbia University's Teachers College and a Bachelors of Business Administration from Bryant College in Smithfield, Rhode Island.

He is on the faculty of the New York University School of Continuing and Professional Studies' Leadership and Human Capital Management department, where he developed and teaches two courses: Creating a High-Performance Workplace and Introduction to Organization Development. Whether with clients or students, he encourages learning through self-reflection and taking actions.

Michael is a member of the New Jersey Organization Development Network and lives in Basking Ridge, New Jersey, with his wife, Carol.

For more information and to download an illustration of the Triangle or the Performance Conversation Surveys, please visit www.mtullassociates.com.

REFERENCES

Adams, Marilee G., *Change Your Questions, Change Your Life*. San Francisco: Berrett-Koehler, 2004.

Argyris, Chris, "Teaching Smart People How to Learn." *Harvard Business Review*, Reprint #91301, May–June 1991.

Block, Peter, *Stewardship*. San Francisco: Berritt-Koehler, 1996.

Bolman, Lee, and Terence Deal, *Modern Approaches to Understanding and Managing Organizations*. San Francisco: Jossey-Bass, 1984.

Bossidy, Larry, and Ram Charan, *Execution*. New York: Crown Publishing, 2002.

Buckingham, Marcus, and Curt Coffman, *First, Break All The Rules*. New York: Simon & Schuster, 1999.

Choppin, Jon, *Quality Through People*. San Diego: Pfeiffer and Company, 1991.

Collins, Jim, *Good to Great*. New York: HarperCollins, 2001.

Conner, Daryl R., *Managing at the Speed of Change*. New York: Villard Books, 1992.

Creech, Bill, *The Five Pillars of TQM*. New York: Plume, 1994.

Csikszenthmihalyi, Mihaly, *Flow*. New York: HarperCollins, 1990.

Dennis, Pascal, *The Remedy*. Hoboken, NJ: John Wiley & Sons, 2010.

Drucker, Peter, *The Practice of Management*. New York: HarperCollins, 1954.

"Employee Engagement, A Review of Current Research and Its Implications." Research Report E-0010-06-RR, The Conference Board, 2006.

Gallwey, W. Timothy, *The Inner Game of Work*. New York: Random House, 2000.

Gottlieb, Marvin R., *Getting Things Done in Today's Organizations*. Westport, CT: Quorum Books, 1999.

Hackman, J. Richard, and Greg R. Oldham, *Work Redesign*. Reading, MA: Addison-Wesley Publishing, 1980.

Hams, Brad, *Ownership Thinking*. New York: McGraw-Hill, 2012.

Herzberg, Frederick, "One More Time, How Do You Motivate Employees?" *Harvard Business Review*, Reprint #R0301F, January 2003.

Hirschhorn, Larry, *The Workplace Within*. Cambridge, MA: MIT Press, 1988.

Katzenbach, Jon R., *Peak Performance*. Boston: Harvard Business School Press, 2000.

Koestenbaum, Peter, and Peter Block, *Freedom and Accountability at Work*. San Francisco: Jossey-Bass/Pfeiffer, 2001.

Kotter, John P., *Leading Change*. Boston: Harvard Business School Press, 1996.

Kouzes, James M., and Barry Z. Posner, *The Leadership Challenge*. San Francisco: Jossey-Bass, 1988.

Liker, Jeffrey K., *The Toyota Way*. New York: McGraw-Hill, 2004.

Mager, Robert, and Peter Pipe, *Analyzing Performance Problems*. Atlanta: CEP, 1983.

Marciano, Paul L., *Carrots and Sticks Don't Work*. New York: McGraw-Hill, 2010.

McGregor, Douglas, *The Human Side of Enterprise*. New York: McGraw-Hill, 1985.

Murphy, Mark, *Hundred Percenters*. New York: McGraw-Hill, 2010.

Parker, Sharon, and Toby Wall, *Job and Work Design*. Thousand Oaks, CA: Sage Publications, 1998.

Pink, Daniel, *Drive*. New York: RiverHead Books, 2009.

Rosenthal, Robert, and Lenore Jacobson, *Pygmalion in the Classroom*. Norwalk, CT: Crown House Publishing, 1992.

Rummler, Gary, and Alan Brache, *Improving Performance*. San Francisco: Jossey-Bass, 1990.

Schaffer, Robert H., *The Breakthrough Strategy*. New York: Ballinger Publishing, 1988.

Senge, Peter, Richard Ross, Bryan Smith, Charlotte Roberts, and Art Kleiner, *The Fifth Discipline Fieldbook*. New York: Doubleday, 1994.

Shaw, Robert Bruce, *Trust In The Balance*. San Francisco: Jossey-Bass, 1997.

Showkeir, Jamie, and Maren Showkeir, *Authentic Conversations*. San Francisco: Berrett-Koehler, 2008.

Sirota, David, Louis A. Mischkind, and Michael Irwin Meltzer, *The Enthusiastic Employee*. Upper Saddle River, NJ: Wharton School Publishing, 2005.

Smith, Douglas K., *Make Success Measurable*. New York: John Wiley & Sons, 1999.

Vaill, Peter B., *Managing as a Performing Art*. San Francisco: Jossey-Bass, 1989.

Weisbord, Marvin, *Productive Workplaces*. San Francisco: Josey-Bass, 1987.